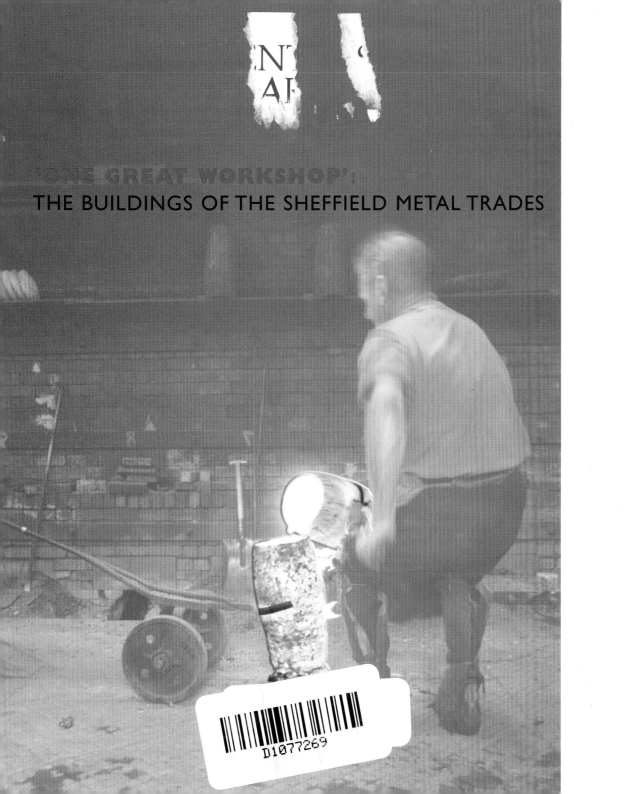

'ONE GREAT WORKSHOP':
THE BUILDINGS OF THE SHEFFIELD METAL TRADES

© English Heritage 2001
Text by Nicola Wray, Bob Hawkins and Colum Giles
Photographs taken by Keith Buck, Tony Perry and Bob Skingle
Aerial photographs taken by Pete Horne and Dave MacLeod
Photographic printing by Keith Buck
Drawings by Allan T Adams
Maps by Philip Sinton
Survey and research undertaken by Victoria Beauchamp, Keith Buck, Garry Corbett, Colum Giles,
Gillian Green, Bob Skingle and Nicola Wray

Edited by René Rodgers and Victoria Trainor
Designed by Michael McMann, mm Graphic Design
Printed by Westerham Press

ISBN: 1 873592 66 3
Product Code: XC20053

English Heritage is the Government's statutory adviser on all aspects of the historic environment.
23 Savile Row London W1S 2ET
Telephone 020 7973 3000
www.english-heritage.org.uk

The National Monuments Record is the public archive of English Heritage. All the research and
photography created whilst working on this project is available there. For more information contact
NMR Enquiry and Research Services, National Monuments Record Centre, Kemble Drive, Swindon
SN2 2GZ. Telephone 01793 414600

Sheffield City Council made a financial contribution towards the publication of this book.

'ONE GREAT WORKSHOP':
THE BUILDINGS OF THE SHEFFIELD METAL TRADES

Text by Nicola Wray, Bob Hawkins and Colum Giles

Photographs by Keith Buck, Tony Perry and Bob Skingle

Photographic printing by Keith Buck

Aerial photographs by Pete Horne and Dave MacLeod

Drawings by Allan T Adams

Maps by Philip Sinton

'One great workshop for the production of cutlery and edge tools – a huge factory which scatters its separate departments in different parts of the town, but still retains them all, like so many links in a chain.'[1]

ENGLISH HERITAGE

Sheffield
City Council

Contents

(left) Crucibles at Abbeydale Industrial Hamlet. The crucibles were made of refractory clay and withstood the intense temperatures of the furnace for only one or two melts. [AA022489]

Foreword

(opposite) The hammer team at Bath Steel Works. [AA022490]

Britain led the world into the Industrial Revolution and, for much of the 19th century, dominated international markets, thanks in no small part to the pre-eminence of Sheffield as a world centre of steel production and cutlery and edge-tool manufacture. For new generations familiar with today's computer- and service-based economy, these achievements may seem distant and scarcely relevant. But Britain's place in global affairs was bought with the skills and energies of its people, and the character of much of its landscape has been formed by its industries.

This book demonstrates how the metal trades of Sheffield affected the lives of its people and shaped the development of the city and its region. It also highlights the fact that despite much change in the city's commercial activity, many examples of industrial buildings survive, as do many of the metalworking skills that gave Sheffield its early industrial impetus. This summation of more than a decade of research arrives at a critical time for Sheffield's future development. Assisted by key stakeholders, the City Council has embarked upon an ambitious drive to increase commercial activity in Sheffield. This initiative coincides with Objective One Funding, a primary aim of which is to encourage investment in the area.

One major challenge for Sheffield is to find ways of keeping industrial buildings in use and earning their keep in a new economic era. All too often, examples of the city's built industrial heritage have fallen by the wayside. Both Sheffield City Council and English Heritage are committed to promoting initiatives that put life back into the industrial buildings that form such an important part of the physical and cultural fabric of the city. In many cases these new applications will be quite different from their original uses, but this approach is more likely to secure the long-term well-being of these buildings. This publication, therefore, should be viewed as both a commitment to the future and a celebration of the past.

Sir Neil Cossons
Chairman, English Heritage

Councillor Peter Moore
Leader, Sheffield City Council

The Sheffield region and the development of the metal trades

Introduction

Fifty years ago every household in the country possessed something made in Sheffield: common tools like spades, saws, planes and chisels; scissors for a multitude of purposes; razors for shaving; a variety of cutting tools, from machetes and the famous Bowie knives to the humble penknife; and the table cutlery used at family mealtimes (Figs 1 and 2). Furthermore, these Sheffield goods could be found all over the world, especially where Britain had built up its Empire. Sheffield was also the nation's major steel producer, supplying the materials for the railway and armaments industries among many others. Together the 'light trades' (cutlery and edge tools) and the 'heavy trades' (steel production, armaments, etc) were of international significance, dominating the local economy and giving employment to thousands of men and women. Today the great industries remain, and steel and cutlery are still produced in large quantities; however, they are no longer the major employers. In their halcyon days these trades created a distinctive industrial landscape, both urban and rural, and the legacy of this period survives at every turn. This can be seen in the form of a unique industrial heritage and in the continuing local pride in the tradition of craftsmanship and enterprise. This book summarises the history of Sheffield's metal trades, describes the processes involved and illustrates the special environment produced by the buildings of the industry.

Topography and resources

Sheffield and its region – known historically as Hallamshire – lie on the eastern flanks of the Pennines (Fig 3). The middle course of the River Don flows south-east until it reaches Sheffield itself, where it turns north-east. In Sheffield and a few miles upstream, the River Don receives the waters of four major tributaries – the Loxley, the Rivelin, the Sheaf and the Porter. The region is one of hills and valleys, dominated today by the built-up area of the city itself but still retaining open land, especially in its western, higher parts (Fig 4).

Fig 1 (top) Unfinished knife blades abandoned in a Sheffield cutlery factory. [AA99/05759]

Fig 2 (bottom) Traditional designs are still used in today's cutlery industry. This United Cutlers design is called 'Fiddle' and is produced in silver and silver plate. [AA022436]

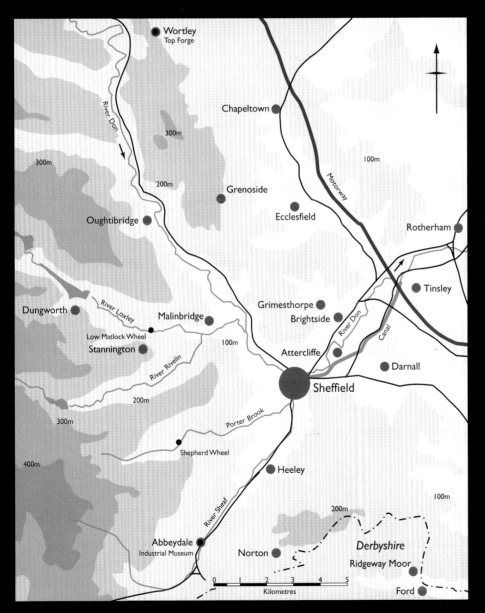

Fig 3 Map of the Sheffield region.

Fig 4 (below) The landscape of the Sheffield valleys: this view of the upper Don valley near Oughtibridge shows the steeply cut, well-wooded hillsides and the scattered settlements where industry and agriculture were combined in a dual economy. [AA022437]

3

Fig 5 One of the waterwheels at Abbeydale Industrial Hamlet. [AA022438]

The metal trades were established in the Sheffield region in the Middle Ages. The natural advantages of the area included local supplies of iron ore and charcoal, the latter used as the fuel for blast furnaces; the availability of local coal, used from the late 18th century in the form of coke to replace charcoal in smelting and forging; good sandstone for grindstones; and, crucially, the steeply falling rivers, which were harnessed for grinding, rolling and forging (Fig 5). Once established, the metal industries encouraged the development of a highly skilled workforce, with knowledge and expertise handed down and developed from generation to generation. This was evident in the 18th century in the local invention of crucible steel and Old Sheffield Plate, and in the 19th and 20th centuries by the invention of a range of special steels for use in the light and heavy trades.

Before the advent of the railways, the topography of the area made communications difficult and Sheffield lay isolated from the main trade routes. The dependence of the industry on supplies of high-quality imported iron (mostly from Sweden) from as early as the 18th century made it imperative to improve on nature in its provision of transport facilities. Water transport first provided the region with its contact with distant sources of supply and markets. The River Don was navigable to Tinsley (3 miles downstream from the city) in the 18th century, and the Sheffield and Tinsley Canal brought water transport into the heart of the town when it opened in 1819. Just two decades later, however, railways provided a more rapid bulk transport system and, from the late 1830s, Sheffield was drawn into the national network, opening up wider markets for its products.

History

Sheffield has been associated with cutlery production since the Middle Ages. Chaucer referred to a 'Schefield thwytel' (a multi-purpose knife carried in a sheath attached to a belt) in *The Reeve's Tale*, and many travellers have been forcibly struck by the special character of the area. In the 16th century John Leland noted the 'many smiths and cutlers in Hallamshire',[2] and early in the 18th century Daniel Defoe observed 'the houses dark and black, occasioned by the continued smoke of the forges, which are always at work'.[3] The importance of the cutlery trades was recognised in 1624 when an Act of Parliament incorporated the

Fig 6 (right) The Cutlers' Hall, Church Street, was rebuilt in 1832 to designs by Samuel Worth and B B Taylor. From this site the Company of Cutlers has regulated the cutlery industry since the 17th century. [AA022439]

Fig 7 (below) Crucible-steel production in the early 20th century. The molten steel is being poured or 'teemed' into a mould, while in the background crucibles dry on shelves against the furnace stack. [Image supplied by Sheffield Libraries, Archives & Information, Local Studies Library]

6

Company of Cutlers (Fig 6), responsible for regulating the cutlery industry in Hallamshire and 6 miles beyond. By the mid-17th century, three out of every five men in Sheffield were employed in cutlery production.

Sheffield took a major step in diversification and consolidation in the late 17th and early 18th centuries when it began to manufacture its own steel rather than relying upon supplies of imported materials. A view of the town in 1737 shows two cementation furnaces, which were used to convert iron into blister steel. What really transformed Sheffield into a major centre of innovation, however, was Benjamin Huntsman's development of crucible or cast steel. Huntsman, a Doncaster clockmaker, felt that a better quality steel was necessary for the manufacture of springs and pendulums, and his experiments resulted in the invention of crucible steel, traditionally dated to 1742 (Fig 7). The new steel was gradually adopted in the manufacture of cutlery and edge tools, giving a better cutting edge, and later in the production of high-quality castings. From the late 18th century Sheffield became the nation's principal producer of various types of steel.

At much the same time that Huntsman was freeing Sheffield of dependence on imported traditional steel, Thomas Boulsover, a local cutler, was laying the foundations of a new industry. In 1743 he fused a thin sheet of silver on to copper to produce silver plate, later known as Old Sheffield Plate. The combined ingot, which could be hammered and worked as one metal, had great commercial possibilities because it was much cheaper than solid silver. From the 1750s a large range of fancy goods such as candlesticks and coffee pots was produced for a middle-class market eager for the appearance of silver at lower cost. Britannia or 'white' metal, a mixture of tin, copper and antimony, catered for the cheap end of the market. A silver trade, which developed as an offshoot of silver plate, was also established in the town by the 1760s. Recognition of the trades came in 1773 when Sheffield and its manufacturing rival Birmingham were permitted to open Assay Offices. Silver plate thrived for around a hundred years before being largely superseded by electroplated goods, patented by Elkingtons of Birmingham in 1840. The first Sheffield electroplate manufacturer was John Harrison, who purchased his licence in 1843, and this branch of the industry came to assume great importance in the town (Fig 8).

Fig 8 A company plaque in Trafalgar Street: evidence of the importance of silver and electroplate production in Sheffield. [AA022446]

The final major development in the Sheffield metal trades was the introduction of bulk steel manufacturing in the second half of the 19th century. Both blister and crucible steel were produced in modest quantities, inadequate for the demands of an industrial economy. Henry Bessemer's 1856 invention of the technique of bulk steel production in his 'converters', together with later improvements that made the technique commercially viable, introduced a new dimension to Sheffield's industrial base. This allowed diversification away from the established emphasis on cutlery and edge-tool production and made it possible to satisfy the demands

of the rapidly expanding railway and armaments industries (Fig 9). Sheffield quickly put itself at the heart of these heavy trades, and the great names of Sheffield bulk steel production – Vickers, Browns, Cammells, Hadfields, Firths and many more – rose to prominence in this period. Constant experimentation in a highly competitive environment led to further developments of major significance, particularly in the production of new alloy steels. These were made in small quantities for specialist purposes using the old crucible-furnace techniques. Stainless steel, invented by Harry Brearley at the Firth Research Laboratory in 1912, was the best known and, for the cutlery industry, the most significant of these alloy steels.

Fig 9 The Bessemer converter introduced bulk steel production to Sheffield. This rare survival comes from Workington and is on display at the Kelham Island Museum. [AA022440]

The organisation of the industry

Within the Sheffield region, a degree of local and trade specialisation developed over the centuries. Some of the outlying villages concentrated on agricultural tools such as scythes (the speciality of Norton) or sickles (made mainly in Eckington), while the cutlery trades tended to be concentrated in Sheffield itself. In 1844 *The Penny Magazine* described Sheffield as one great workshop, 'which scatters its separate departments in different parts of the town, but still retains them all, like so many links in a chain'. [4] This apt allusion highlights the fact that Sheffield was involved in all aspects of metalworking, from primary steel production through to manufacturing the finished articles, and the manner in which this was undertaken.

Trades and the stages of production

Steelmaking was a highly skilled and technical operation and it demanded considerable capital investment. From the late 17th century Sheffield became a steel producer and ultimately manufactured a range of steels for a variety of purposes. In the 18th and 19th centuries the steelmaker might produce blister steel in cementation furnaces and then refine it using the crucible process. Both blister and crucible steel required further processing prior to the manufacturing of goods. This was achieved by power forging (also known as hammering or 'tilting') or rolling, which shaped the steel into bars and gave it a closer grain and strength. The blister steel especially benefited from this process, which removed impurities and produced 'shear' steel, a more uniform material with a combination of flexibility and the capacity for holding a sharp cutting edge. Re-forging the shear

steel further refined it to produce the world-renowned 'double-shear'. Steelmakers often produced steel both for their own purposes and to be sold on to the trade. In 1862 Firths advertised as manufacturers of files, saws and edge tools and as makers of a wide range of steels. This practice continued into the era of bulk steel production.

Steel was the starting point for the manufacture of a huge variety of cutlery and agricultural edge tools, and a lengthy sequence of processes was necessary to attain a high-quality finished product. The first stage in cutlery production was the hand forging of blanks, but some edge tools, such as crown scythes, were forged again to weld a strip of crucible steel between two pieces of wrought iron (Fig 10). After forging, a cutlery or edge-tool blade needed a sharp cutting edge prior to assembly into a finished item. Blades were ground by hand on a grindstone powered by water, and later by steam, gas or electricity (Fig 11). The final stage of the manufacturing process was the assembly of the component parts. This often included the fitting of a handle to the blade and finishing the article ready for sale. Handles were made from a wide variety of materials such as silver, ivory, horn, wood, mother-of-pearl and porcelain, depending upon the type and quality of blade being produced.

The expertise acquired in these primary manufacturing processes was exploited in a variety of allied trades such as the manufacture of Old Sheffield

Fig 10 (left) Scythes and sickles on display at Abbeydale Industrial Hamlet. Abbeydale was used for the manufacture of scythes. [AA022441]

Fig 11 (below) Grinders, astride their 'horses', at work in a typical grinding hull in the early 20th century. [Image supplied by Sheffield Libraries, Archives & Information, Local Studies Library]

9

Fig 12 Fletchers, Arundel Street. Modern silver-cutlery production uses traditional methods and is still based on the skills of the craftsmen and women. [AA99/09162]

Plate, silver, electroplated and Britannia metal goods (Fig 12). Much fancy tableware was pressed into shape using drop stamps and dies, which were particularly useful for stamping electroplate and Britannia metal goods. A range of products, from buttons and combs to horn powder flasks, was manufactured using the knowledge obtained through working with materials used for handles. Other notable associated trades included file cutting (vital to the cutlery and edge-tool industries), the manufacture of stove grates, the spinning of 'hollow ware', and leather work such as the production of razor strops and the coverings for buffing wheels (so named because of the use of buffalo hide as a covering).

The organisation of production

Before the 19th century most cutlers operated on a small scale and, except for steel production, were involved in every aspect of manufacture from forging and grinding their own blades to assembling the finished items. The trades that required power, such as power forging, rolling and grinding, were at first situated along one of Sheffield's five rivers, often in rural locations. The concentration of such water-powered sites was matched in few other areas of Britain. By the late 18th century the River Don had an average of 3 water-powered sites per mile, the Loxley and Sheaf had 4, and the Porter and Rivelin had 5 and 6 respectively. Water-powered grinding workshops (known as wheels) were provided by landowners, notably the lords of Hallamshire (the Earls of Shrewsbury and later the Dukes of Norfolk).

Before the 19th century unpowered processes, such as hand forging, file cutting and assembly, were carried out on a small scale in the workers' own homes or in workshops. There is little physical evidence for early sites, but the Hearth Tax returns of 1672 show that there were 600 smithies within a 10-mile radius of Sheffield. Rural metalworkers practised a dual economy of farming and metalworking, but in the town, with its 224 smithies (one to every 2.2 houses), artisans probably worked full time in the cutlery trades, albeit from small workshops.

The 18th century saw the development of specialised working. For example, grinding became a distinct full-time trade and some specialist grinders worked entirely within one aspect of the industry such as cutlery or saw blades. This division of labour affected other trades as well. By the early 19th century all aspects of cutlery and edge-tool manufacture (forging, grinding, hardening, tempering, hafting (handlemaking) and assembly) were highly skilled specialisms. Many independent craftspeople worked on only a single stage of production, such as table-knife forging or penknife assembly. Articles often circulated around the town between different artisans, who each completed their part of the manufacturing process before passing it on for the next stage.

By the late 18th century some water-powered sites like Abbeydale Works had developed a measure of integration, allowing a greater degree of control over production (Fig 13). Growing demand, from both domestic markets and a rapidly expanding overseas market (particularly the United States), encouraged integrated factory production. From the 1820s a number of large steam-powered works such as Globe Works were built in the town to respond to new opportunities (Fig 14). When Sheaf Works was built in 1823 the intention was of '... centralising on the spot all the various processes through which iron must pass...until fashioned into a razor, penknife or other article of use'. [5] Steam power released the manufacturers from dependence on riverside locations and enabled them to set up in town, close to the market and transport infrastructure. The typical large works henceforth employed steam power for processes such as heavy forging,

Fig 13 (above) Abbeydale Industrial Hamlet is a valuable educational resource and a perfect illustration of how integrated edge-tool production was housed in the 19th century. In view (from the right) are cottages and offices, the grinding wheel, the forge and the crucible shop. [AA022442]

Fig 14 (left) Globe Works, Penistone Road: one of the new integrated cutlery factories built in the early 19th century. The Classical-style offices face the street and workshops are located at the rear. [AA022443]

grinding and stamping. They combined this with facilities for steelmaking and workshop accommodation for the hand processes that remained central to high-quality cutlery and electroplate production (Fig 15). The new national and international standing of the cutlery industry was reflected in the establishment of London showrooms by the larger Sheffield firms, and these showrooms acted as the shop window for the region's goods.

Increased production was not entirely dependent on the building of integrated factories, for at the same time a large number of smaller works were built in the town and its hinterland. Usually consisting of loose groupings of workshops around a yard, these provided accommodation for a single company or for a multitude of small manufacturers each renting a room or rooms (Fig 16). The cutlery trades were thus drawn together into a mutually advantageous proximity, largely replacing the fragmented domestic production. The construction of these

Fig 15 (above) Cornish Works, Cornish Place: a former electroplating factory. The large chimney shows how sizeable works such as this depended on steam power in the 19th century. This works has been converted to office and residential use. Cleaning has brought out the attractive colour of the brickwork. [AA022444]

Fig 16 (right) Workshops at Beehive Works and, in the background, Eye Witness Works, both on Milton Street. [AA022445]

small, unpowered works demonstrates again the cutlery trades' reliance throughout the 19th century on the traditional hand skills that gave the city its reputation for high-quality products. In 1879 it was said that 'the highest excellence can be attained only by the employment of intelligent hand labour'. [6]

Alongside the expanding industry located in the city, the surrounding countryside continued to play an integral part in the growth of the metalworking trades. The majority of surviving, rural hand forges and small workshops are 19th century in date and thus are contemporary with the urban sites (Fig 17). Most have no associated agricultural buildings, indicating that by the mid-19th century many metalworkers were not dependent on a supplementary income from farming. The rural craftspeople often undertook wholesale work for, and sold their products to, the urban merchants and manufacturers for retail to the public.

Although some of the large cutlery firms employed substantial numbers of workers in the 19th century, many of them subcontracted work out to independent makers known as 'Little Mesters'. These independent makers paid the works owner for their workspace, possibly employed one or two hands to help them and took on work both from the factory owner and other makers. The retention of such a system was a reflection of the domestic roots of the industry, the highly skilled nature of the work involved and the fact that it offered advantage to both the large-scale manufacturers and the artisans. The manufacturers were able to respond quickly to a specialist and perhaps short-lived demand without requiring large capital investment, and the craftspeople enjoyed the freedom to work for any employer and were not at the mercy of a single company's fortunes.

The Old Sheffield Plate and electroplate industries were different from cutlery and edge-tool production in that they were urban and factory-based from their inception. This was probably because they involved high initial costs beyond the means of small, rural, independent cutlers. The monetary value of the goods also meant that close attention needed to be paid to security, which was easier if the various processes were gathered together in one location. Electroplate factories varied in size: the largest was Cornish Works, which opened in 1822, while the small works at 16–20 Sidney Street represented a more modest level of operation. Direct employment was used in the large silver and electroplating works, probably as a security measure; for example in 1906 James Dixon employed over 900 people at Cornish Works.

Fig 17 The file-cutting workshop at 11 High Street, Ecclesfield. The need for good light is indicated in the provision of long windows. Internal shutters gave security at night. [AA98/14081]

13

The heavy trades, including bulk steel production and the manufacture of products such as armour plating, guns, rails and axles, grew rapidly from the middle of the 19th century. Their growth was encouraged by the introduction of new methods of steelmaking, the development of a good transport system and the rapidly expanding national and international market for their products, especially during the international arms race and in wartime. They formed the apex of Sheffield's industrial pyramid, employing thousands of workers in the great works that developed alongside the railway and canal in the Lower Don Valley (Fig 18). In 1916, at the height of war production, Vickers had 11,000 workers at its River Don Works. Direct employment was used for steel manufacturing, which

14

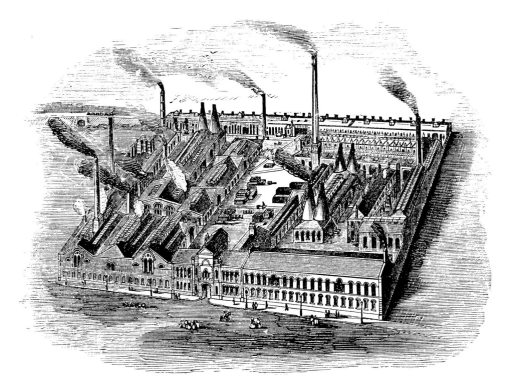

Fig 18 Atlas Works, Savile Street, 1862. Now largely demolished, John Brown's factory, begun in 1857, was one of the group of large steel works in the Lower Don Valley. Elaborate offices faced the street, while grouped behind were cementation and crucible furnaces, forges and all the buildings required to produce not only steel but also a range of articles such as armour plate and railway springs. In 1862 Atlas Works had two Bessemer converters, together capable of castings weighing 7 tons. [Image supplied by Sheffield Libraries, Archives & Information, Local Studies Library]

required large capital investment and sizeable teams of workers to operate the furnaces and forges. However, here too there was a subdivision of processes. It was unusual for a firm to have the facilities for all stages of steel production and even the largest firms sent steel out for rolling and power forging, an arrangement known in Sheffield as 'hire-work'. This cut down on outlay and allowed rapid turnover and flexibility in taking on new work.

The metal trades of Sheffield and its region showed immense variety in a constantly changing picture. They produced everything from penknives to 80-ton guns; operated from small rural forges and from factories covering many acres; provided employment for the small independent craftspeople; and brought riches and public recognition to the great steelmasters. The organisation of the industry was highly complex, and the workshops and factories that housed the many trades still reflect this complexity and provide the area with its distinctive character.

Buildings, works and working conditions

Individual metalworking processes were variously housed. Rural and urban buildings and powered and unpowered sites had specific characteristics determined by the nature of the processes that they accommodated. This section describes the different building types and demonstrates how they were grouped within works complexes. It also examines the working conditions commonly encountered in the metal trades.

Primary steel processing

Cementation and crucible furnaces, used for the production of steel for cutlery and edge-tool manufacture, are very distinctive in appearance, and perhaps more than any other building type symbolise Sheffield's association with the metal trades. The cementation or converting furnace was the earlier type – present in Sheffield from the early 18th century – and was used to convert iron into blister steel. This process took several days and involved packing bars of Swedish iron between layers of charcoal in two sealed sandstone chests so that they could absorb extra carbon during the firing process. The furnace was brick-built, conical

Fig 19 (right) Cut-away view of a cementation furnace. The low-arched opening gives access to the furnace, which is built around two large sandstone 'coffins'. In this view the further coffin is packed with bar iron and charcoal and the nearer one awaits filling. The complex flue structure around the coffins is evident in this view.

Fig 20 (below) Baltic Steel Works, Effingham Road. This 1862 view shows cementation and crucible furnaces grouped at the rear of the site. [Image supplied by Sheffield Libraries, Archives & Information, Local Studies Library]

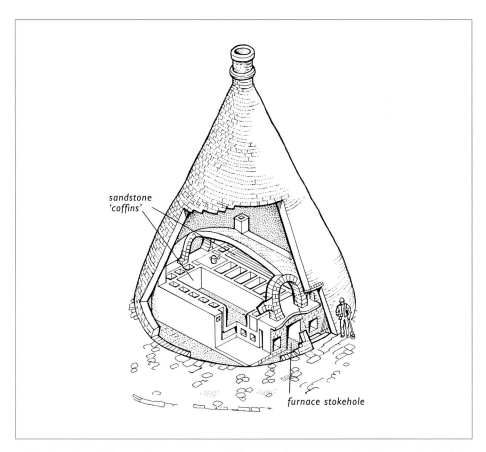

sandstone 'coffins'

furnace stokehole

or bottle-shaped like a glass or pottery kiln, and from 35 to 60ft (11 to 18m) high (Fig 19). Furnaces were usually contained within a workshop building, also used for the storage of materials, with the upper part of the furnace chimney projecting out of the roof. They were often built in groups of two or more, particularly within large integrated factories like Baltic Steel Works (Fig 20). Only one cementation furnace survives in Sheffield today in anything like substantial form (Fig 21), but 19th-century illustrations reveal how dominant they once were as part of Sheffield's skyline (Fig 22). The introduction of bulk steel-production methods began the process of gradual obsolescence of cementation furnaces,

Fig 21 (left) Doncasters Cementation Furnace, Doncaster Street, is the only cementation furnace standing in Sheffield. It is a Scheduled Ancient Monument. [AA012791]

Fig 22 (below) Sheaf Works, Maltravers Street, in the mid-19th century. The works was established in 1823 as the first integrated cutlery factory in the town, and included a fine pedimented office and warehouse block (now a pub), a steam-power plant, ranges of workshops and a large cluster of cementation furnaces. [Image supplied by Sheffield Libraries, Archives & Information, Local Studies Library]

17

Fig 23 Cut-away view of the Abbeydale crucible furnace. The melting shop is raised above a brick-vaulted cellar. The melting holes can be seen next to the long rectangular stack. In the left foreground is the pot shop where crucibles were made.

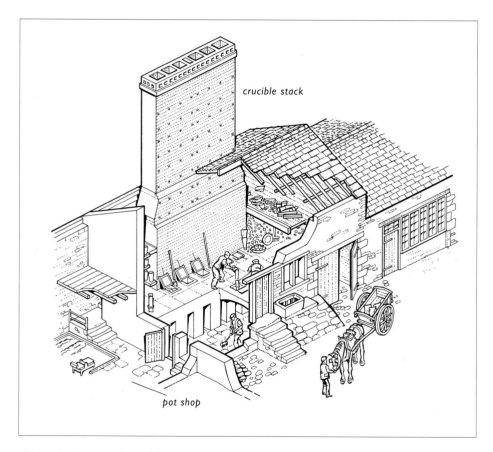

crucible stack

pot shop

although they continued in use in diminishing numbers as late as World War II and beyond.

Blister steel was made into higher grade crucible steel in crucible furnaces. Pieces of blister steel, often with other ingredients, were packed into preheated crucibles of highly refractory clay and the recipes were kept as closely guarded secrets. The crucibles were heated at up to 1600°C for around three hours, dispersing the carbon and freeing impurities. The crucibles were then lifted out of the melting holes, the slag was skimmed off and the molten steel was poured or teemed into moulds by hand (Fig 23). This process was also found suitable for

Fig 24 (far left) The last commercial melt in a Sheffield crucible furnace. This 1971 photo shows how the charge from two crucibles could be combined before teeming when a casting of some size was required. [© Bob Hawkins]

Fig 25 (near left) Part of Darnall Works: the interior of one of the small crucible shops on Wilfrid Road. The shop was lit by unglazed, shuttered windows and skylights. The crucible stack at the rear retains brackets for the shelves where crucibles were dried, but the melting holes in the floor have been covered. [AA022447]

19

making a range of special steels, produced in small quantities for specialist uses. The highly particular form of the buildings that housed crucible-steel production meant that the crucible furnaces fell into disuse when other methods of production were developed. The last commercial 'melt' took place in the 1970s (Fig 24).

Crucible-furnace units often comprised a pot shop, where clay was trodden and the crucibles made (before the 19th century each crucible could only be used for two or three melts); a charge room, for preparing and weighing raw materials; and a single-storey melting shop containing both the melting holes (one for each crucible) and an open space for teeming the steel into the ingot moulds (Fig 25). The intense temperature required to melt the blister steel demanded a strong draught, so melting shops were built with large cellars and tall chimneys. The wide rectangular stacks, immediately identifiable, were built of brick. At their bases, where the heat was greatest, sturdy horizontal metal bands provided additional strength. Higher in the stacks, iron ties strengthened the flue structure. The form of the chimney lent itself to use as an end wall or as part of a rear wall of a melting shop.

Fig 26 (near right) The crucible furnace at Abbeydale Industrial Hamlet. The iron ties securing the flue structure can be seen in the large stack. [AA022448]

Fig 28 (far right) No. 35 Well Meadow Street: a mid- to late 19th-century works. In the foreground is the crucible stack, with louvered ventilation openings, iron strengthening to the base and metal ties in the upper wall. The small manufacturer's house is situated beyond the workshop range and works entrance. [AA022450]

20

Fig 27 (below) Pluto Works, Princess Street: a small, late 19th-century crucible-steel works. The furnace lies to the left with the one remaining stack visible on the far gable. Other buildings include offices and, on the street corner, probably a forge for reworking the cast metal. [AA022449]

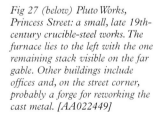

Surviving urban melting shops are generally small brick buildings housing six to twelve melting holes, but the crucible furnace at the once rural Abbeydale Works is stone built with a brick stack (Fig 26). Melting shops were commonly lit by large round-headed or segmental-arched windows and by skylights over the working area. Windows were originally shuttered and unglazed with wooden cross-frames and vertical metal bars, providing security and ventilation to disperse the heat of the furnaces. Roof trusses were often carried on masonry or iron corbels to prevent deterioration of the timber caused by excessive heat. Iron brackets, attached to the furnace stack, once supported crucible-drying shelves.

Melting shops were constructed in a variety of forms. They could be built as small, specialist steel works such as Pluto Works (Fig 27); in conjunction with a single manufacturing process like file cutting, as at 35 and 54 Well Meadow Street (Fig 28); or as part of integrated factories like Baltic Steel Works. Integrated sites tended to have both crucible and cementation furnaces, although this was by no means invariably the case. In the second half of the 19th century some of the large works had a number of furnaces providing hundreds of melting holes. Sanderson's Darnall Works, which originally had a total of 180 melting holes, is the only remaining example (Fig 29). It has a row of five small melting shops in a range broken up by the large, transverse crucible stacks, and, at a right angle, a substantial melting shop with 52 melting holes, which could be used for the production of large castings.

Fig 29 (top left) The large melting shop at Darnall Works, Darnall Road. Forming a single working area internally, the shop had 52 melting holes, contained in 12 stacks, 6 of which are seen rising through the roof. [AA022451]

Fig 30 (top right) Cyclops Works, formerly Cammells, Carlisle Street. This factory now principally consists of large, brick-fronted, corrugated-steel sheds of the early 20th century. It was used for the manufacture of armour plate and, until recently, retained large presses. [AA022452]

Fig 31 (left) A press at work in John Brown's Atlas Works in the early 20th century. The press was contained within a typical steel-framed shed. [Image supplied by Sheffield Libraries, Archives & Information, Local Studies Library]

The techniques of bulk steel production were taken up by the heavy trades and used for the manufacture of guns, shells, plate and rails. The main requirement, in terms of accommodation for these later methods of steelmaking, was space to house the bulky machinery. The building became simply a shell that sheltered a processing area and it might be used for any of a number of heavy processes such as steel production, rolling and pressing plates, heavy forging and

Fig 32 (above, left) The Gun Shop (formerly Firths), West Gun Works, Savile Street. Built in 1863–4, it represents the type of large brick building required in the substantial factories of the Lower Don Valley in the middle decades of the 19th century. [AA022453]

Fig 33 (above, centre) The dominant features of the Lower Don Valley in the 20th century were the corrugated-steel-clad sheds that housed most of the processes in the great steel works. Few of these sheds survive today. This example forms part of the River Don Works, formerly Vickers and now Sheffield Forgemasters. [AA022454]

Fig 34 (above, right) Low Matlock Wheel: rolling titanium for the aerospace industry. The heated metal is being passed through the rolls to reduce it to the required dimensions. [AA022455]

materials (Fig 32). Roofs were constructed of fireproof metal trusses, often with skylights to provide additional illumination and ridge louvres for ventilation. These brick buildings have largely been replaced by the great black corrugated-steel-clad sheds, which were so characteristic of the Lower Don Valley in the 20th century (Fig 33).

Powered processing: forging, rolling and grinding

The powered processes, which harnessed the abundant resources of the local river system, determined the location of the cutlery industry in and around Sheffield. Forging, rolling and grinding were central to the region's economic development, and their remains, therefore, have a great importance today.

Forges and rolling mills were awesome places when in full production, with the senses battered by heat, smoke, thunderous noise and movement. They fulfilled the similar functions of refining and processing iron and steel before use in cutlery and edge-tool production. They needed power to drive the huge tilt and forge hammers in forges and the stands in rolling mills, furnaces to reheat the metal prior to forging or rolling, and a well-lit uncluttered workspace with wide openings for the movement of goods. Bulky machinery meant that buildings were generally large, particularly in the case of rolling mills, which also required a substantial working area (Fig 34). Power forges were expensive buildings to

construct and fit out, and a degree of architectural pretension was often present in earlier examples as a show of confidence and self-advertisement to customers (Fig 35).

Before the middle decades of the 19th century forges were water-powered, with the power being used to drive not only the hammers but also the bellows to produce a draught for the furnace. The remains of the water-power system and hammers survive at Mousehole Forge, an evocative ruin on the River Rivelin. Top Forge at Wortley and the forge at Abbeydale Works on the River Sheaf are preserved largely intact. Both have large reservoirs providing a good supply of water for the wheels. Top Forge has a main rectangular range that houses the hammers and an aisle to the rear where the furnaces were originally located (Fig 36). This arrangement kept the main working space clear for the movement of raw materials and finished articles, a process aided by the use of jib cranes.

Fig 35 (top) Abbeydale Industrial Hamlet. The large gabled buildings with Venetian windows house the forge (left) and grinding hull (right). Between them are the waterwheels which power the workshops. [AA022456]

Fig 36 (left) The tilt hammer at Top Forge, Wortley. The waterwheel can be seen outside the building. The forge is maintained by the South Yorkshire Trades Historical Trust and is open to the public. [AA022457]

Abbeydale has a smaller forge with two hammers (Fig 37), but the same principle of keeping a clear working space was achieved by recessing the furnace into a side wall and placing the waterwheels for the hammers and furnace blower outside the building.

Steam had distinct advantages over water power. It allowed a free choice of site location and was capable of almost infinite expansion, especially important in the development of the heavy trades. In the middle of the 19th century the traditional tilt hammers began to be superseded by steam hammers, which were developed by James Nasmyth in 1842 and were capable of delivering precisely controlled blows of great power. A new type of forge with larger buildings began to be built, which looked much like those housing bulk steel-producing facilities. Some steam hammers are still in use in Sheffield, but they are now powered by compressed air. At Bath Steel Works, there are four large hammers of different weights, housed within a tall, single-storey brick forge (Figs 38 and 39). Unglazed, shuttered windows and skylights illuminate the working area. Gas-fired furnace hearths are situated around the edge of the working space, which is covered with rectangular metal plates to guard against fire and to help in the dragging of metal

Fig 37 (below, left) The tilt hammers in the forge at Abbeydale Industrial Hamlet. The large spur wheel, which turns the drive shaft working the hammers, can be seen in the background. [AA022458]

Fig 38 (below, right) The 30 hundredweight hammer in action at Bath Steel Works, Penistone Road. A team of three (a first hand or 'cod', a hammer driver and a furnace man) operate the hammer. [AA022459]

24

Fig 39 (left) Iron tools ready for use at the furnace and hammers at Bath Steel Works. [AA022460]

Fig 40 (above) Low Matlock Wheel. The 1882 rolling mill was powered by water drawn from the River Loxley and falling on the overshot wheel to the right. [AA022461]

from the furnace to the hammers. Powered forging was also undertaken on a smaller scale within steam-powered, integrated works producing articles for the light trades. Nineteenth-century engravings of processes such as table-blade and file forging show that small tilt and steam hammers could be used in a workshop with no effect on the form of the building other than the provision of mechanical power to drive the machinery.

Rolling mills require a large amount of space to allow the passage of long steel bars through the rolling stands. A good surviving example is Low (or Little) Matlock Wheel in the Loxley Valley (Fig 40). On a site first used in the 1730s, the present mill dates from 1882 and retains its waterwheel, which is set outside

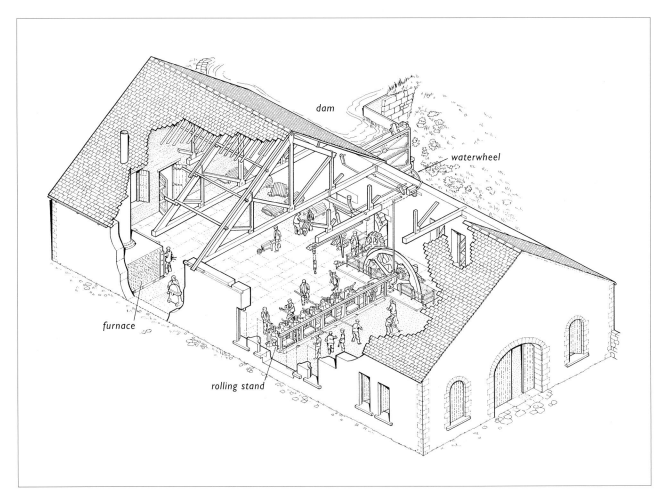

dam

waterwheel

furnace

rolling stand

Fig 41 The 1882 mill at Low Matlock Wheel. Steel bars, stored in one corner of the building, are heated in the furnace and then rolled in the stand, which is driven by the waterwheel.

the building. The mill is a lofty, single-storey building with ample room internally for the furnaces (now gas-fuelled), the rolling stands that reduce the bars to the required dimensions and the working areas (Fig 41). Rolling mills could operate either as independent businesses or within integrated cutlery works. The heavy trades employed large steam engines to drive rolling and pressing mills capable of producing armour plating over 300mm thick.

Fig 42 (far left) Cyclops Works, Carlisle Street: the interior of the large, early 20th-century shed, now empty of equipment. The structure of the shed was independent of any machinery and simply provided a shelter for processing. Travelling cranes permitted the movement of heavy castings. [AA022462]

Fig 43 (near left) The grinding hull at Shepherd Wheel: a late 18th-century water-powered workshop on the Porter Brook. One of the grinding troughs, with the grindstone and the 'horse' on which the grinder sat, is in the foreground. The belt drive from the main drive shaft and the gearing from the waterwheel can be seen in the background. The building is maintained by Sheffield Industrial Museums and is open to the public. [AA022463]

27

The River Don Works rolling mill was powered by a 3000hp engine, now on display at the Kelham Island Museum. By the early 20th century rolling in the large works of the Lower Don Valley was commonly housed within the sort of all-purpose shed which accommodated the heavy processing that made up their business (Fig 42).

Specialist grinding workshops, known as 'wheels', were built from as early as the 16th century and most were controlled by the estate of the Dukes of Norfolk and the other major landowners. The grinding wheels, powered by water before the 19th century, produced the cutting edge on which the reputation of the industry depended. Two restored water-powered wheels remain intact in Sheffield. Shepherd Wheel, a site on the River Porter, was developed in the 16th century as a grinding wheel by the lords of the manor of Sheffield and was expanded in the late 18th century. Another grinding wheel, built in 1817, survives as part of Abbeydale Works on the River Sheaf. Both wheels are wide, single-storey buildings constructed of local sandstone with stone slate roofs in the local vernacular style. Although the closely spaced windows are now glazed, they were probably open originally to aid ventilation. Both buildings have a typical arrangement of machinery inside, with the grindstones closest to the windows in order to benefit from the good light and the glazing wheels (used for finishing the blades) situated towards the rear of the 'hull' or grinding room (Fig 43).

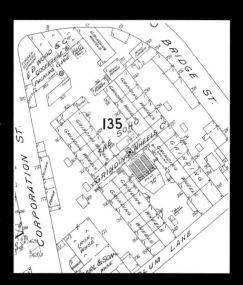

Fig 44 (above) Soho Grinding Wheel. This 'public' wheel provided four ranges of grinding hulls and a central power source.

Fig 45 (right) Sellers Wheel, Arundel Street: a medium-sized cutlery works built in the mid-19th century. The front range provided offices and workshops, and the rear block housed grinding hulls on both the ground floor and part of the first floor (note the blind walls pierced only by small openings for ventilation) with well-lit workshops above. [AA022464]

By the 19th century two types of wheels were differentiated – the 'public' wheel and the 'private' wheel. Public wheels were built as commercial speculations. They were devoted exclusively to grinding, provided the necessary power and machinery for this trade and were available for rent (Fig 44). Some of the urban examples could be very large and required steam power. Soho Grinding Wheel had 50 grinding hulls and accommodated 500 grinders, while Union Works had grinding hulls on two floors. Grimesthorpe Steam Grinding Wheel, perhaps the last of these specialist works, was recently demolished. It was constructed around 1840 to the north-east of the town centre, with back-to-back grinding hulls and a central steam engine house.

Private wheels formed part of a works in which other manufacturing processes were carried out, but facilities were often available for rent, with whole rooms or separate troughs (for grindstones) being let to grinders. The grinding hulls were set on the lower floor or floors of the workshop ranges, and they were lit by large, closely spaced windows throwing light onto the grindstones. They often had brick jack-arched ceilings to support the weight of the upper-floor hulls and sometimes had ventilation grilles in the rear wall to extract some of the extremely harmful dust produced by the grinding process (Fig 45). Before the late 19th century most urban grinding wheels were powered by a small steam engine. A line shaft ran along the back of the grinding hulls and a belt drive linked this line shaft to each individual trough.

Unpowered processes

Much of the work involved in cutlery and edge-tool production was carried out using hand power in workshops. The hills around Sheffield once echoed to the sounds of industry, and the surviving small workshops of vernacular character

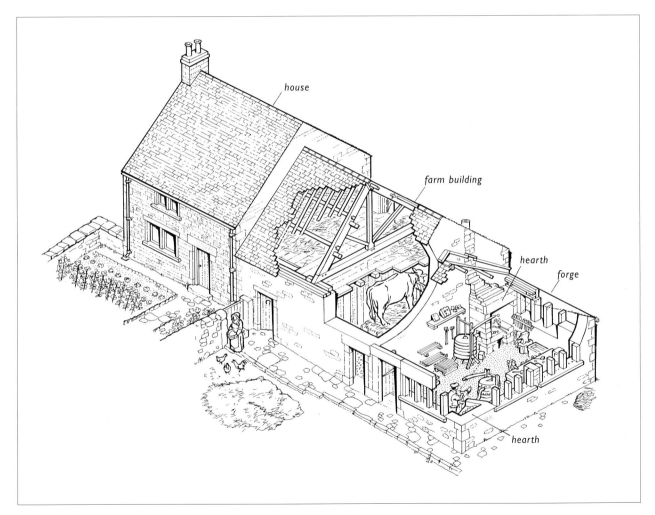

house

farm building

hearth

forge

hearth

demonstrate the cottage scale of this rural trade, largely devoted to the production of agricultural tools. At Sykehouse, Dungworth, a forge with two hearths forms part of a range of structures including a house and farm buildings. This grouping illustrates how the dual economy – agriculture and industry – survived into the 19th century (Fig 46). The rural forge at Franklin Cottage, Nook Lane,

Fig 46 Cut-away reconstruction of Sykehouse, Dungworth. The forge has hearths in opposite corners and is lit by windows in three walls.

Fig 47 (top) The early 19th-century hand forge at Franklin Cottage, Nook Lane, Stannington, is a rare survival of the once-common rural workshop in which craftspeople made a living producing edge tools like scythes and sickles. [AA022465]

Fig 48 (bottom) The interior of the file workshop at 11 High Street, Ecclesfield. The files were cut on the stone blocks set beneath the windows, which could be secured at night by lowering the internal shutters. The room contained hearths for working the metals. [FF000791]

Stannington, also has two hearths and a generous working space where the stithy (anvil) and stock would have stood (Fig 47). File workshops were a distinctive and important building type in rural areas, and can be identified by the long windows required for lighting the intricate process of cutting the files. A good example is the early 19th-century workshop at 11 High Street, Ecclesfield (Fig 48). In this workshop, a fireplace with two hearths was used for softening the files, which were then cut on eight equally spaced stone blocks. As well as the file workshop, the complex included a house, farm buildings and a forge.

Small hand forges were also very common in the town, but few now remain. Most surviving hand forges form part of integrated cutlery works and date from the mid-19th century. They were often built in rows on the ground floor of multi-storeyed workshops. Each forge comprised just a single room with space for only a furnace, an anvil and a small amount of working room. These sites are easily identifiable externally, not only by the individual entrances to each room, but also by the common combination of a stable-type split door and an adjoining casement window sharing a wooden frame under a single lintel (Fig 49). Another type of urban hand forge was described at Alma Works, Barker's Pool, where 'instead of being each a small separate building, as used to be the case, [they] are open to each other for the purpose of ventilation through the whole length of the building, without anything to break the free current of air' (Fig 50). [7]

Fig 49 (below, left) A small hand forge on the ground floor of a workshop range in Portland Works, Randall Street. The forge shows the typical feature of the combined door and window under a single lintel. [AA022466]

Fig 50 (below, right) The open hand-forge range at Cyclops Works in the mid-19th century. This view shows the operation of hand forging on a large scale in Cammell's factory in the Lower Don Valley. [Image supplied by Sheffield Libraries, Archives & Information, Local Studies Library]

31

32

Fig 51 (above) The small cutlery works at 57 Garden Street has two- and three-storey ranges of workshops around a small yard. [AA022467]

Fig 52 (right) A typical yard view in a Sheffield cutlery factory. The large number of flues served hearths inside the workshop. [AA022468]

Workshops were the dominant building type in the metal trades and were used to house the mainly hand-powered processes involved in the assembly and finishing of goods and for associated trades such as electroplating and handlemaking. They sometimes stood alone on tiny urban plots, forming miniature works run by independent Little Mesters (Fig 51). Others formed part of integrated cutlery factories. Often hidden behind a modest office block on the street front, they were invariably utilitarian brick ranges, usually from two to four storeys in height (Fig 52). Many of the workshops were very narrow in depth and were housed under a mono-pitch roof. This plan may have resulted from the restrictions imposed by small urban plots, but it also allowed the penetration to all

parts of the interior of good light, necessary for the fine work involved in cutlery production. Large and closely spaced wooden-framed windows pierced the yard elevation. Where the workshops were not combined with grinding hulls or forges, floors were of timber, despite the fact that most workshops had a large number of hearths used to heat metals. The flues for these hearths rose above the eaves of the yard elevation in some workshops and above the higher rear wall in others (Fig 53). The documentary sources make it clear that the workshops were often in multiple occupation, even within some of the larger integrated works, and one might expect to see evidence for the provision of segregated access (Fig 54). However, this is usually encountered as an adaptation, and access, segregation and security must have been very much an *ad hoc* matter, with working spaces divided according to ever-changing circumstances.

The development of factories for cutlery and silver-plate production

The expansion of trade from the late 18th century led to the construction of a range of factory types. Some of these were on a scale unprecedented in Sheffield, while others continued the almost domestic operation characteristic of earlier centuries. Early integrated rural works that manufactured agricultural edge tools might have included a complete range of processing buildings. Abbeydale, for example, comprises a crucible furnace, a tilt with forge hammers, a grinding

Fig 53 (above, left) Stag Works, John Street, is one of the larger silver and electroplating works. It has well-lit workshops with a large number of flues rising from the eaves and from the rear of the mono-pitch roofs. [AA022469]

Fig 54 (above, right) Workshops at Beehive Works. The steps give independent access to the first-floor shops and may indicate that the range was designed for occupation by a number of Little Mesters. [AA022470]

33

Fig 55 The triumphal arch giving access to Henry Hoole's foundry. Built in 1860, the arch displays panels depicting Hephaestus and Athene. [AA022471]

wheel, hand forges, workshops and offices. The first fully integrated cutlery factory in the town was Sheaf Works, built by William Greaves in 1823 alongside the recently opened Sheffield and Tinsley Canal. Early integrated factories made their own blister and crucible steel on site and also carried out the subsequent manufacturing processes: for example Greaves turned his steel into a wide range of products including razors, penknives and table cutlery. These factories formed substantial complexes with batteries of furnaces and large ranges of forges. A steam plant provided the power for processes such as forging and grinding, and workshops were grouped around a series of yards. The large scale of investment was reflected in the construction of impressive Classical-style offices on the display frontage. Perhaps the most imposing factory entrance survives at the Green Lane Works iron foundry, where a triumphal arch, built in 1862, carries a clock tower above the roofline and gives access to the yard (Fig 55).

After 1850 primary steel production was excluded from many larger, centrally located cutlery factories such as Beehive Works and Eye Witness Works; instead, supplies of steel were either bought in or produced on other, less central, sites. As a result, these later complexes, less varied in their buildings, were essentially groupings of workshops used for the lighter trades associated with cutlery production. Workshops, offices and other buildings were grouped around one or more yards, with the overall plan dictated by the shape of the plot. Perhaps because men of lesser capital built them, these urban cutlery works had more modest office buildings on the street frontages, where quiet dignity replaced the grandeur of earlier works (Fig 56). A cart entrance gave controlled access to the yards for both the workforce and goods, and the yards provided a secure space for the unloading and loading of goods. In built-up urban settings the yards also acted as light wells for the buildings around their perimeter. The modest requirement for mechanical power meant that a steam plant might have been accommodated in the yard, with perhaps a small engine housed in a corner of one of the workshop ranges. Furnaces and the noisier, heavier processes, such as grinding and forging, were commonly located at the rear of the site. The less noisy processes such as assembly, finishing and packing were conducted towards the front in order to minimise disturbance to the offices and showrooms. In this way, articles moved logically through the manufacturing processes towards the front range where they were stored.

35

Fig 56 Butcher's Wheel, Arundel Street: one of the larger town-centre cutlery factories. [AA022472]

Fig 57 (above, left) Anglo Works, Trippet Lane: a small cutlery works comprising a single workshop building with an office at one end. [AA022491]

Fig 58 (above, right) No. 35 Well Meadow Street is a small file works, with buildings grouped around a stone-paved yard. The crucible furnace is in the corner, under the long catslide roof with skylights. [AA022473]

Fig 59 (opposite, top left) Venture Works, 103–5 Arundel Street, was built in the late 18th century as part of a row of houses, but was rapidly taken over for industrial use with the addition of workshops at the rear. Until recently, Herbert M Slater made a wide range of knives here. [AA022474]

Smaller urban complexes were built at the same time as the large integrated factories. Some of these, like Anglo Works, consisted of little more than a single range of buildings, often with an office at one end (Fig 57). Other complexes, involved in only a restricted range of processes, nevertheless incorporated buildings around a small yard. At 35 Well Meadow Street these buildings include a small crucible furnace, with file workshops grouped around it (Fig 58). Within respectable residential areas, overtaken by the march of industry – for example Lambert Street and Arundel Street – some houses were converted for industrial use. Venture Works originated in the late 18th century as the northernmost of a terrace of three brick-built houses, but by 1888 the house and added workshops were used as a tenement factory by six separate businesses, all connected to the cutlery industry (Fig 59).

The development of electroplating and Britannia metal industries in the early 19th century led to the construction of a number of new factories. Cornish Works became one of the largest electroplating concerns, similar in scale to the more substantial cutlery works. The importance of the firm was reflected in the display frontage to Green Lane (Fig 60). Within the complex there were several workshop

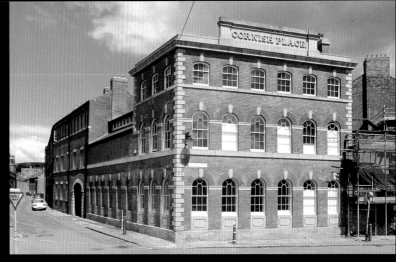

Fig 60 (top right) James Dixon's Cornish Works, near Kelham Island, has a well-detailed mid-19th-century office block on the main-approach elevation. [AA022475]

Fig 61 (bottom right) The plating shop at Cornish Works has distinctive large windows and clerestorey lights. [AA022476]

Fig 62 (bottom left) Truro Works, Matilda Street, was a Britannia metal factory. It has been successfully converted to residential accommodation, retaining all the principal buildings around yards of irregular shape. [AA022477]

ranges grouped around yards and also buildings unique to the electroplating trade such as the large plating shop (Fig 61). Smaller electroplating establishments were similar to cutlery works, and many of the processes were conducted in the type of all-purpose workshop range found in cutlery factories. At Truro Works typical ranges were tightly grouped around inner and outer yards (Fig 62), and in the

Fig 63 (above) The small electroplate works at Nos 16–20 Sidney Street has a front range with offices and a two-storey workshop to the rear. [AA022478]

Fig 64 (right) Stan Shaw is one of the few remaining craftsmen making knives by traditional methods. Almost like an 18th-century cutler, he undertakes every process, from forging and grinding through to final assembly, and operates from a small workshop in Garden Street. [AA022492]

modest works at 16–20 Sidney Street there were simple two-storey front and rear ranges divided by a small yard (Fig 63).

The typical Sheffield works changed almost from year to year, with a bewildering succession of occupiers of different trades and an almost continuous process of addition and alteration. A good example is Leah's Yard, Cambridge Street, which began as a small works used for the manufacture of shears and other tools early in the 19th century. Over the course of the 19th century, it housed a number of occupiers, including a horn dealer (who supplied the handlemaking trade), silver platers, knife manufacturers and silver stampers. The buildings show evidence for innumerable additions and alterations; perhaps the most significant change of the late 19th century was the introduction of steam power, used to run a grinding hull and drop hammers in a silver die-stamping shop. The key features of Leah's Yard, as of so many other works, were the adaptability and the intensive development of the site. It provided a type of accommodation that could be used by a number of trades within the metal industries and exploited the site to the limits of its capacity by crowding buildings into a confined space to provide flexible, affordable, but not necessarily convenient, working spaces.

Working conditions

The craftsmen and women working in the Sheffield metal trades were highly skilled. Knowledge and equipment were passed down through the generations, even up to the present day. The few remaining skilled workers continue to use the tools and methods developed centuries ago (Fig 64). Despite this craft base,

39

Fig 65 (above, right) No. 35 Well Meadow Street: a typical workshop interior with benches under the windows. A firm of scissors manufacturers used this shop most recently. [AA022479]

Fig 66 (above, left) Women were mainly occupied in the lighter trades in cutlery production. In this photo, 'buffer girls' finish cutlery by using polishers driven by a belt drive from an overhead line shaft. [Image supplied by Sheffield Libraries, Archives & Information, Local Studies Library]

however, cutlery production has never been a highly rewarded occupation. The early working conditions for most people were at best basic, with indescribable filth building up in cramped and poorly equipped workshops. In what might have been one of the better works in the 1860s, one cutler described conditions as 'crude and sordid: makeshift buildings, shops and closets ... The dirty shops, the disregard of sanitary demands, and the arbitrary way the workmen were treated, all tended to low ideals of life' (Figs 65 and 66). [8]

For many trades, conditions were not only squalid but also extremely hazardous, and workers risked death on a daily basis. Though the combination of molten metal and heavy machinery had obvious dangers, other manufacturing processes were more deadly. In particular grinding and file cutting had sinister reputations. Grinding was commonly known to be the most injurious of the metalworking trades since there was always a danger of a stone bursting due to a fault. There was also a serious problem with the dust from grinding, which gave the workers silicosis or 'grinders' lung', considerably shortening their life span. Despite the awareness of the problem in the 19th century, it was not until the late 1920s that legislation was imposed making employers liable to pay compensation to workers who had contracted silicosis.

File cutting was an equally dangerous trade. Once file teeth had been cut on one side, the file was turned over in preparation for cutting on the reverse side. In order to protect the finished side, the file was placed on a block of soft metal made up of a mixture of lead and tin. File cutters, therefore, were very susceptible to lead poisoning. Throughout the 19th century in Sheffield, hand cutting of files continued despite the invention of file-cutting machines, since it was believed that handwork resulted in a superior product.

While there is understandable pride in the triumphs of Sheffield's industrial achievements and in the city's reputation for craftsmanship, it must be acknowledged that success came at a price. The industry was dirty and Sheffield came to share some of this character. Many of the trades were hazardous and took a heavy toll on the health of the workforce. Amelioration of both environmental conditions and common working practices were among the primary concerns of reformers in the 19th century. Change was slow, however, and could never eliminate some of the dangers inherent in an industry such as steel production.

The landscapes of the metal industries

The late 20th century saw a significant adjustment in Sheffield's economy as the service sector took over from manufacturing as the leading employer. This change is expressed most dramatically in the drawing power of the Meadowhall shopping centre, built in the 1990s on the site of Hadfield's great steel works. Despite this transformation, the remains of industrial activity are still sufficiently prominent to give Sheffield a particular character, seen in both rural and urban contexts.

The rural landscape – with its buildings and settlement pattern, communications, water management systems, quarries and woodland – has been shaped by the demands and consequences of the metalworking trades. This is

Fig 67 Low Matlock Wheel from the air. The rolling mill, located in a bend of the River Loxley, nestles in the bottom of the wooded valley. [NMR 17574-14]

41

illustrated most dramatically by the intensive exploitation of Sheffield's rivers. The sheer volume of sites is difficult to imagine nowadays, but the evidence for buildings and water systems, such as leats, dams, weirs, sluices and so on, comprises an intricate network of remains, revealing the importance of the industry in the countryside. Where water-powered sites survive in substantial form an impression can be gained of the nature of the rural industry. At Low Matlock Wheel, the rolling mill, dam, offices and cottages form a small grouping that nestles in the valley and is isolated from other settlements (Fig 67). Abbeydale Works is of international distinction, not only because it retains most of its buildings as a 'time capsule', but also because it represents a significant development in integrated working. What is lacking in the rural landscape,

Fig 68 (above) Sykehouse, Dungworth, with its combination of house, farm building and forge, is a reminder of how domestic industry once flourished in the cutlery trades. [AA022480]

Fig 69 (right) 'The Big Chimney' by Joseph Pennell, 1909. This illustration shows a view across Sheffield with the River Don dimly visible in the foreground. [Courtesy of Sheffield Galleries & Museums Trust]

however, is the equivalent of the textile mill village – often constructed by the mill owner – with housing and other buildings clustered around the factory. The structure of the metal trades, which was characterised by many independent operators who employed perhaps a few hands in small works close to existing settlements, made the provision of this type of site unnecessary, and it was certainly beyond the means of most rural cutlery manufacturers.

The hand forges and workshops scattered throughout the surrounding villages complemented the water-powered wheels and were built on a far more modest scale. In 1830 William Cobbett observed that 'the ragged hills all around this town are bespangled with groups of houses inhabited by working cutlers'. [9] This pattern of dispersed settlement with numerous smallholdings could have resulted from the system of dual occupation that prevailed in early times. Sykehouse, Dungworth, a smallholding with a small forge, highlights the survival of a dual economy into the 19th century (Fig 68). Remaining workshops act as important reminders of the strong rural engagement in industry. In Hoyland Swaine, three nail-making shops survive within the gardens of a row of terraced houses, and the file-cutting workshop at 11 High Street, Ecclesfield employed perhaps a dozen people. The sheer number of these workshops, perhaps in the hundreds, demonstrates that a significant part of the rural working population gained their livelihood from metalworking rather than from agriculture.

The town of Sheffield, assailing the senses with the evidence of industry, made a forcible impression on visitors from the 16th century onwards. In 1989 one retired cutlery worker described the city as 'one big boom, boom, boom, like a big heart going…all exciting and alive', [10] and this was also true in earlier centuries as well. Less acceptable than the reverberation of heavy machinery was the smoke, noted by Defoe in the early 18th century. In 1841 another visitor called Sheffield 'one of the dirtiest and most smoky towns I ever saw'. [11] The furnaces and chimneys of the factories produced a permanent smog. In *The Road to Wigan Pier*, George Orwell described Sheffield in the 1930s: 'Once I halted in the street and counted the factory chimneys I could see; there were thirty-three of them, but there would have been far more if the air had not been obscured by smoke' (Fig 69). Even the names of the factories – Cyclops, Atlas, Pluto, Aetna and many others – identified the area with the workings of a Herculean industry.

Some areas and streets still give an impression of the former dominance of the

Fig 70 Central Sheffield, showing the location of many of the city-centre sites mentioned in the text.

1   Bath Steel Works, Penistone Road

2   Globe Works, Penistone Road

3   Cornish Works, Cornish Place

4   Green Lane Works, Green Lane

5   Doncasters Cementation Furnace, Doncaster Street

6   Well Meadow Street

7   John Watts Cutlery Works, Lambert Street

8   Anglo Works, Trippet Lane

9   Beehive Works, Milton Street

10 Eye Witness Works, Milton Street

11 Kenilworth Works, Denby Street

12 Stag Works, John Street

13 Portland Works, Randall Street

14 Truro Works, Matilda Street

15 Nos 16–20 Sidney Street

16 Lion Works, Arundel Street

17 Sellers Wheel, Arundel Street

18 Butcher's Wheel, Arundel Street

19 Venture Works, Arundel Street

20 Sheaf Works, Maltravers Street

21 Cyclops Works, Carlisle Street

22 Baltic Steel Works, Effingham Road

23 Pluto Works, Princess Street

24 Gun Shop, West Gun Works, Savile Street ('Gripple')

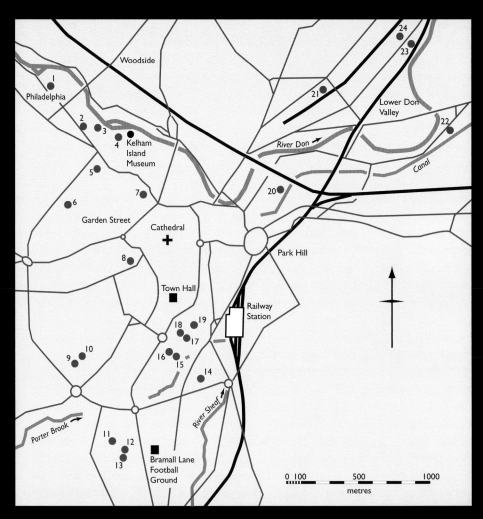

metal trades (Fig 70). The grouping of factories around Kelham Island, such as the refurbished Cornish Works, Wharncliffe Works, Green Lane Works and Globe Works, comprises one of the most impressive concentrations of industrial buildings (Fig 71). They form memorable streetscapes, especially when the views take in the River Don, which some factories overlook. In the Lower Don Valley,

the canyon formed by the buildings of the River Don Works on either side of Brightside Lane gives an impression of the scale of the larger factories (Fig 72). The survival of pubs alongside the large steel works is a reminder that small beer was the preferred means of slaking thirst for workers in the factories (Fig 73), but almost all the housing has been cleared. Despite the scale of many of the urban steel and cutlery factories, there is little evidence that the factory owners in Sheffield provided housing and other facilities for their workforces. The absence

Fig 71 (top right) The landscape of Sheffield's metal trades: a view of the Kelham Island area showing a saw and file factory, a foundry, Cornish Works, and steel and cutlery works. The weir across the River Don feeds water into a headrace, a reminder that water power was once important even in Sheffield itself. [NMR 17567-11]

Fig 72 (top left) The Vickers factory, River Don Works, in Brightside, is the largest surviving steel-castings enterprise and is now operated by Sheffield Forgemasters. The office and design block was built in 1907 and its size reflects the huge scale of the Vickers' business. [AA022481]

Fig 73 (bottom left) The typical association of steel works and corner pub, well placed to serve a thirsty workforce. Here the Wellington public house is located directly beside the entrance to the River Don Works. [AA022482]

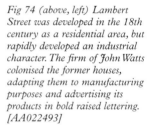

Fig 74 (above, left) Lambert Street was developed in the 18th century as a residential area, but rapidly developed an industrial character. The firm of John Watts colonised the former houses, adapting them to manufacturing purposes and advertising its products in bold raised lettering. [AA022493]

Fig 75 (above, right) This aerial view of Milton Street shows how two of the most complete cutlery factories have yards and ranges of workshops behind the street frontage. [NMR 17567-18]

Fig 76 (right) The John Street/Randall Street area near Bramall Lane: a densely built-up development, with Portland Works in the foreground and Stag, Harland and Clifton Works behind. [NMR 17567-12]

of this provision echoes the situation in the rural industrial landscape. In Sheffield, therefore, speculators were primarily responsible for this infrastructure.

Closer to the city centre, the eccentric street elevation of the John Watts Cutlery Works is an exercise in advertising (Fig 74). Milton Street, with its long frontage consisting of Beehive Works and Eye Witness Works, is more restrained but still impressive (Fig 75), and the area around John Street, near Bramall Lane, shows how densely packed parts of the city once were (Fig 76). Arundel Street retains much of its former industrial character and incorporates a variety of buildings: Venture Works (originally a house); Sellers Wheel and Butcher's Wheel (both integrated cutlery factories including grinding hulls); and the diminutive Lion Works, a rare

surviving example of a small workshop range incorporating an office at the street end. Even where cutlery works survive in isolation, they are important contributors to the urban scene. The significance of the smaller establishments should not be overlooked: for example Kenilworth Works is a reminder of the key role played by lesser companies in the highly complex organisation of the metal trades (Fig 77).

The emblematic structures associated with early steel production are of special importance in Sheffield's landscape. There were once over 200 cementation furnaces in the city, making a major impact on visitors with their discharge of dense smoke. Only one now remains in substantial form. Recent excavations on the site of Jessop's Brightside Works revealed the bases of a number of furnaces, emphasising how this phase of Sheffield's industrial past can now be recovered only through archaeology (Fig 78). Sheffield has almost all the surviving English examples of crucible furnaces. This building type, above all others, makes the landscape of the metal trades distinctive and represents the birth of the modern steel industry. The furnace at Abbeydale Works, which retains all its fittings, forms part of the industrial museum (Fig 79), but all other furnaces are either derelict or used for other purposes. The range of multiple furnaces at Sanderson's Darnall Works, which is the only surviving example of large-scale production of crucible steel anywhere in the world, is of particular significance.

Fig 77 (above, left) Kenilworth Works, Denby Street, was originally built as a comb works, but it is typical of the smaller cutlery works that were once so common. The entrance arch gives access to a small yard and a rear workshop range. [AA022483]

Fig 78 (above, centre) Excavations at Jessop's Brightside Works in 2001 uncovered the remains of cementation furnaces. The outline of the two sandstone 'coffins' can be seen within the enclosing wall of the circular furnace. [AA022484]

Fig 79 (above, right) The crucible shop at Abbeydale Industrial Hamlet survives with all its tools and equipment and vividly illustrates how crucible steel was produced. [AA022485]

The rarity of both cementation and crucible furnaces and their significance in terms of industrial innovation give the remaining buildings an interest beyond their very utilitarian form.

Sheffield's metal industries were of international significance. They combined high-quality manufacturing with mass production and underpinned Britain's maintenance of a great trading empire. These industries were diverse but intricately interrelated, and these characteristics were evident both in the remaining buildings and the rural and urban landscapes. The humble workshop as well as the great integrated works played a crucial role in the region's metal trades. The subdivision of linked processes meant that products often travelled the breadth of the town during their manufacture. Consequently, all buildings, whether part of a complex or housing a single process, are crucial to our understanding of how the metal trades operated and evolved. The legacy of industry provides a resource of huge importance; skills have been retained in the cutlery industry and new industries have built on the traditional association with metalworking. Also important, however, is the way in which the remains of industry help to define the region's identity, giving it a unique character and image.

The future of Sheffield's industrial heritage

The conservation management of Sheffield's industrial heritage presents a formidable challenge, and the scope of this task has been highlighted by the recent English Heritage survey of surviving industrial buildings in the Sheffield region. The survey, which examined a great many of the surviving sites, revealed that in spite of economic decline and much demolition there remains an extraordinary variety and spread of sites. It has provided the means of understanding the national and international significance of Sheffield's historic industrial buildings and supplies the context for future conservation strategies aimed at sustaining their special character.

In the late 19th century Sheffield was one of the world's most influential industrial cities. Underpinning its manufacturing base was the quality of the steel it produced, literally giving it the 'edge' over rival producers – a superiority on which the city's cutlery and edge-tool industries have traded ever since. Sheffield's products and its metallurgical knowledge were exported throughout the world. Although other countries developed bulk steelmaking industries, which were to outstrip Sheffield in terms of quantity, the city's reputation for the range and quality of its special steels was not significantly challenged. At the end of the 20th century, however, extreme changes in manufacturing patterns within the global steel industry caused great upheaval and the loss of many jobs. The cutlery and edge-tool industries have experienced decline and shrinkage of both markets and workforce and have adapted less successfully to changed circumstances. Nevertheless, the cachet of 'Made in Sheffield' still underpins the city's steel industry, and today this industry makes almost as much steel as it did at its peak in the 19th century, with only a fraction of the former workforce.

The physical legacy of Sheffield's industrial might was the vast array of buildings spreading the length and breadth of the city and overspilling into the rural hinterland in all directions. The constant renewal and expansion of a highly specialised building stock – much of it specific to a single trade and some integrating steelmaking and metalworking processes – characterised the development of this great industrial community. Today, in spite of the extensive clearances associated with recent changes, a unique range of industrial buildings survives and a few examples of almost all of the major processes and trades are preserved in some form or another. This built legacy includes the rural hand forges of farmer-sicklesmiths, water-powered grinding hulls, rolling mills, crucible steel furnaces, file-cutting shops, integrated steel and tool works, cutlery factories and electroplating works. Almost all of these are visually distinctive, as the processes taking place inside shaped their external appearance.

These buildings were often grouped together, but the renewal of large parts of the city has meant that the intimate environment of the city's densely-packed industrial heart – with houses, churches, pubs and schools interspersed with forges, furnaces and workshops – has been weakened. Pockets of predominantly 19th-century industrial buildings survive in several parts of the city and provide areas of a distinctive historic character. Sheffield City Council has long recognised the importance of the metal trades to the city; as early as the 1960s it gave far-sighted support for the preservation of two internationally significant sites,

Fig 80 Despite some losses, Arundel Street retains important groupings of cutlery works, including the large Butcher's Wheel and, opposite, the smaller Sellers Wheel. [NMR 17567-19]

Abbeydale and Shepherd Wheel, both now industrial museums. More recently Kelham Island and the grid of streets formed by the Duke of Norfolk's Arundel Street development (now known as the 'Cultural Industries Quarter') have been designated as conservation areas by the Council (Fig 80). Pride in the city's unique metalmaking and metalworking skills still remains high, but the interest of many of its historic industrial buildings is not widely recognised yet.

Important first steps in securing the future of the city's historic industrial buildings and sites are the recognition and validation of their special interest and the provision of a framework for their future management. Unlike the rapid development of 19th-century Sheffield, today's changes are regulated by the planning system. There are three main strands to the planning framework that shape the way in which decisions are made about the historic environment. First, nationally significant sites where long-term preservation is feasible, especially where below-ground remains survive, can be scheduled as **Ancient Monuments**. Second, **Listed Buildings** legislation allows us to recognise and protect individual buildings of 'special architectural or historic interest'. Careful research and survey work underpin the recommendations we make to central government to list buildings or schedule monuments and allow us to provide descriptions that accurately portray the special interest of industrial building types previously unrecognised as nationally significant. The listing of buildings of special interest often supports the third strand of statutory protection – the creation by local authorities of **Conservation Areas**, the character and appearance of which it is desirable to preserve or enhance.

Once sites and areas are officially designated, local plans and government guidance inform the way in which they are managed. The intention of both listing and conservation area designation is to ensure that the site's special interest is given proper consideration when change, whether alteration or new development, is envisaged. Without these means of managing change, far fewer of Sheffield's distinctive industrial buildings would have survived to the present day and the coherence of conservation areas would have been eroded by the gradual loss of the building stock. Neither listing nor conservation area designation is intended to prevent all change, nor to rule out creativity or imagination in the search for a solution to a building's needs. Both can be used to prevent unnecessary demolition, unsuitable and insensitive alteration, and new development that fails to respect its surroundings. They allow Sheffield's historic assets to be managed in the best interests of the whole community.

There is a growing recognition that the regeneration of historic buildings can be a major factor in helping to bring about sustainable development in areas such as Kelham Island, where viable businesses sit next to empty premises in various states of decay. Investment in key historic buildings, such as the conversion to residential and commercial use of the electroplating works of James Dixon at Cornish Place, has not only secured the long-term future of a major historic complex, but has also re-focussed attention on the environmental assets of the

51

Fig 81 (right) Cornish Works. A substantial workshop range, including die-stamping shops on the lofty ground floor, lines the River Don frontage. [AA022494]

Fig 82 (below) The row of crucible shops lining the Wilfrid Road frontage to Darnall Works is a unique survival. Despite having been unused for some years, the shops are still substantially intact. [AA012790]

River Don in the heart of the city (Fig 81). Most importantly, projects such as Cornish Place have shown that a future exists for even the largest of industrial sites.

The Sheffield survey has provided a clear picture of what survives and of the importance of those survivals in both local and national contexts. We now know what remains of an industrial environment of international significance and are able to assess the potential for the future use of its surviving buildings. Some of these have lain unused for a considerable period of time and are extremely fragile (Fig 82). Many remain in use, however, and with careful management can have a long and useful future. They also bear witness to the region's unique history. These buildings are often plainly detailed and functional in appearance, but when changes of use are proposed they deserve the same careful attention to detail as is afforded to more obviously 'architectural' structures. Window patterns, internal detailing, plan form and features – the size, number and positions of hearths and chimneys, for instance – are all important to an understanding of how an industrial building works and what gives it its special character.

The challenge ahead – for the City Council, English Heritage, building owners and everyone concerned about Sheffield's unique legacy – is to find a means of keeping the region's industrial buildings in use, earning their keep as working structures and serving as physical reminders of Sheffield's past. With timely and realistic action, these buildings can take their place at the heart of the regeneration agenda. There are already notable success stories in place for emulation and example. Cornish Works is used for both office and residential purposes; Truro Works has been converted into student accommodation; and the Gun Shop at West Gun Works provides light and spacious premises for manufacturing (Fig 83). These successes demonstrate that historic buildings and sites can accommodate change and renewal. Through imaginative and cost-effective schemes, they are able to provide both environmental and economic benefits.

Fig 83 Successful new use of an industrial building: the Gun Shop is now used for the manufacture of wire fence tensioners, exported all over the world. [AA022487]

53

The survival of this legacy of industrial buildings will depend upon co-operative and co-ordinated action by all parties. A determination to preserve buildings still capable of beneficial use and to safeguard their special qualities will need to be matched by a creative approach to their adaptation. A programme is required to identify and designate sites and areas worthy of protection; to secure the maintenance and repair of neglected sites; to provide detailed guidance on potential new uses and sources of financial assistance; and to help owners to develop sensitive schemes of adaptation. This work has already begun. English Heritage and Sheffield City Council share a commitment to ensure that Sheffield's unique industrial heritage plays its part in the regeneration of the city. It can contribute its distinctive characteristics to the creation of vibrant, sustainable environments and help to provide the new homes and jobs that will re-shape the city's future.

Notes

1 Anon 1844 'A day at the Sheffield cutlery works'. *The Penny Magazine* no. 775, new series, vol 13, supplement, 161

2 Quoted in Hey 1998, 17

3 Rogers, P (ed) 1971 *Daniel Defoe: A Tour Through the Whole Island of Great Britain.* Harmondsworth, 482

4 *See* Note 1

5 Hunter, J 1869 *Hallamshire: The History and Topography of the Parish of Sheffield in the County of York.* Sheffield (revised edition by Arthur Gatty), 174

6 Pawson, H and Brailsford, J 1879 *Illustrated Guide to Sheffield and the Surrounding District.* Sheffield, 253

7 Pawson and Brailsford 1862, 158

8 Quoted in Tweedale 1995, 162–3

9 Quoted in Hey 1998, 111

10 Quoted in Tweedale 1995, 6

11 Quoted in Hey 1998, 102

Further reading

Barraclough, K C 1989 *Sheffield Steel.* Sheffield (reprint)

Bayliss, D (ed) 1995 *A Guide to the Industrial History of South Yorkshire.* Redruth

Crossley, D (ed) 1989 *Water Power on the Sheffield Rivers.* Sheffield

Hey, D 1998 *A History of Sheffield.* Lancaster

Pawson, H and Brailsford, J 1862 *Illustrated Guide to Sheffield and Neighbourhood.* Sheffield (reprinted 1985, Otley)

Tweedale, G 1995 *Steel City: Entrepreneurship, Strategy and Technology in Sheffield 1743–1993.* Oxford

Places to visit

Kelham Island Museum, Alma Street, Sheffield S3 8RY (0114 272 2106)

Abbeydale Industrial Hamlet, Abbeydale Road South, Sheffield S7 2QW (0114 236 7731)

Shepherd Wheel, Whiteley Woods, Sheffield (Open by special appointment, book through Abbeydale Industrial Hamlet on 0114 236 7731)

Wortley Top Forge Industrial Museum, Forge Lane, Thurgoland, S Yorks S35 7DN (0114 288 7576)

Millennium Gallery, Arundel Gate, Sheffield S1 2PP (0114 278 2600)

Cutlers' Hall, Church Street, Sheffield S1 1HG (Access by special arrangement, 0114 272 8456)

(Front cover) Butcher's Wheel, Arundel Street. [AA022495]

(Inside front cover) Atlas Works, Savile Street, 1862. [Image supplied by Sheffield Libraries, Archives & Information, Local Studies Library]

(Inside back cover) Hephaestus with the armour of Achilles. Green Lane Works entrance. [AA022488]

(Back cover) The last commercial melt in a Sheffield crucible furnace. [© Bob Hawkins]